"Having spent fourteen years on Guemes Island, I've come to believe that every island ought to have a mountain. Lummi Island has one. And just as islands need mountains, each distinct place deserves to have a writer who pays attention, who identifies the details which make that place different from all others. Luther Allen has become that kind of writer for Lummi Island, and his book has become, in words, the island's other mountain. *The View From Lummi Island* is a day-book spanning an entire year and, as this poet has written, 'the island and the mind encircle one another, whisper back and forth.' That 'mindful silk' is the fabric of this book."—James Bertolino, author of *Finding Water, Holding Stone*

# The View from Lummi Island

*a journal of excursion into place*

Poems

**Luther Allen**

Other Mind Press ≈ Bellingham, Washington

 First edition.

ISBN 978-069201116-4
Library of Congress Control Number: 2010935116

The cover monoprint, *Lummi Island*, by Luther Allen, with many thanks to the guidance and studio of Sheila Sondik.

Quote from *The Way to Rainy Mountain*, by N. Scott Momaday, Copyright © 1969 University of New Mexico Press. Used with permission.

This book may be purchased from www.villagebooks.com, the Lummi Island Heritage Trust, or in person from the author. For more information: http://othermindpress.wordpress.com.

Once in his life a man ought to concentrate his mind upon the remembered earth . . . He ought to give himself up to a particular landscape in his experience, to look at it from as many angles as he can, to wonder about it, to dwell upon it. He ought to imagine that he touches it with his hands at every season and listens to the sounds that are made upon it. He ought to imagine the creatures there and all the faintest motions of the wind. He ought to recollect the glare of moon and all the colors of dawn and dusk.

—N. Scott Momaday

Yes, but not *just* imagined, or remembered. Experienced, touched.

≈ ≈ ≈

## Author's Notes

For the sake of clarity in the poems, orcas denotes Orcas Island and *orcas* denotes the species of whale.

August 31 through September 7 is a connected series of poems that attempts to pull together a cosmology of nature and consciousness.

My hope is that the reader will have the time and inclination to read this book over the span of an entire year. Many of the poems are seasonal. Pace is important.

ALDEN BANK
PATOS ISLAND
SUCIA ISLAND
MATIA ISLAND
NORTH
BARNES I.
CLARK I.
EAST SOUND
MT. CONSTITUTION
ORCAS ISLAND
ORCAS ISLAND

NOOKSACK RIVER
SANDY PT
LUMMI INDIAN RESERVATION
GOOSEBERRY POINT
PT. MIGLEY
BELLINGHAM
FERRY
BELLINGHAM BAY
VILLAGE PT.
LEGOE BAY
LUMMI ISLAND
HALE PASSAGE
PORTAGE I.
LUMMI ROCKS
ELIZA ISLAND
VITI ROCKS
SINCLAIR I.
CYPRESS I.

For the inhabitants of Lummi Island, 1996-2003,
and beyond.

## January 1

last night:
bonfire on the beach
friends in firelight
oysters, posole, red wine . . .

commingling with
        cloud-muted stars
        the damp wind of this season
        and the slap and shush of the water

wrapping us around
the entire world

## January 2

yeah, and it's a good thing
we met last night.

now: cold
wind-driven rain,
a pelting darkness

find a blanket, a book.
no one is talking.

sleep, not fire
draws us, holds us
in this long night of winter

## January 3

this island
smoothed and settled
humped and wild

thrown just off
the exploded heart
of the san juans

## January 4

to the west:

grey layers and violet lines
smeared fractals and escher covenants
holding/creating     sweeping away
stalwart islands and thin-skinned waters
spasmodic winds and
skittish, fragile beliefs.

## January 5

to the north:

the unseen flattening
fraser delta

jagged abrupt bulkhead
of bc mountains

and beyond:
grizzly, caribou, greyling

and just a bit further:
white seas, white bears

white fantasy.

## January 6

to the east:

all intent
governed, overwhelmed
by pale ephemeral apparition
of mount baker

the center of the earth, revealed
still restless

the sacred fear.

## January 7

to the south:

the lorelei
the teeming exigency
the inevitability

of seattle.

## January 8

winter here:

shrunken days     wrenched into a grey core
cold squish on dank inverted soil
all the plants down
to bare stalk and prayer

dripping

except the rogue blackberry     of course
still leafed and thorned
crouched, gathering
for spring wars

## January 9

i forget—
in other places
are there stars
in winter?

is the moon more
than a slight muddled glow
diffused through grey clabber
more imagined, remembered
than real?

## January 10

late night wait at ferry landing
mainland side
heron hunts shallows
in eerie pier lights

believing every night
is full moon

## January 11

no such fool
is the wood duck
decoy
nailed to the piling
on the opposite landing

it has transcended
believing
thinking, even eating—
just waits
and watches

## January 12

black water cold and flat
like a vast, honed stone

white snow
crazed skeltering flakes
as big as sparrows

blanket and suffocate
the shrunken cosmos
of this day's dusk

feeding the darkness.
nothing more, nothing less.

## January 13

at this season
smells are bare
close to the bone

salt-strung shore
rotting kelp
chalky scrape of clam shell

and sometimes the smell of just
cold wet grey

and from farther out
the smell of long purple-green swells
wafts of shearwater, wingtips just wet

and from farther still
(paul and colleen's big goatdog drools)
pit roasted pig, somebody's supper
in hawaii

## January 14

freshly battered tree trunk on the beach
scarlet orange bark shatters through
the thousand tints of winter grey:

ornament

## January 15

ribbed clouds
pearled light

the mud
burnt umber
slick
frigid

holding
neat and paired
the half-moon pooled
tracks of deer

## January 16

the cats
—hopefully just darwin's soldiers—
neatly place
mouse and mole cadavers
stiff carcasses of birds
on the steps

as if gifts

## January 17

encased in the wet of grey
interlaced layers of ooze
the earth, the sky

and in the end
in the beginning
at all edges:

the sea

## January 18

prescient and scattered
slurps and slaps of quiet waves on rock

—like that stretched little moment
when the orchestra winds down its tuning
and remnant peeps and moans diminish
before full storm
orchestration.

## January 19

season of high tides, storms,
all the beaches rearrange,
trade logs, flotsam

sending messages, sculpting
in their own eternal, practiced
way.

## January 20

we ponder
and work so hard
our raveling of this world

comes down to:

eagle flies
fish dives

but sometimes
not fast enough.

## January 21

reflected shimmer
hovering flaxen

way off
in front of matia:

as close as the sun
gets today

## January 22

the violent thrust
of mt baker
flanked by
the ever-attendant sisters
the litter of the cascades

now the spreading foundation
of our sunrise vista

secured, calmed
by thirty foot blanket
of snow

## January 23

mind:

> popsnap of round cobble on beach
> slip on salt-smeared algal bedrock
>
> two ducks bob through wind-wrecked waves
> two tugs blow spray into the far heavens

nothing more

## January 24

matia crouches out there
slavering in the one small crumb of sunshinc
its worn rocky shores
extended like paws, resting
stretching
getting ready to yawn

## January 25

wind, wind

> shoving waves, splattering crests
> churning litter of clamshells, bits of crab, sundered chitons
> punching down snowberry thickets
> tearing through firs

finally

> ripping away
> my last thoughts

## January 26

(ferry ride)

WHUMP!

tons of metal thud and shudder
vehicles wrack uneasily against their brakes
barrels of saltwater dump on windshields

wild unrelenting southeast wind
straight up hale's passage
building fierce determined waves

wrestling chaotically under the floating
placid and wan
effortless and silent

moon

## January 27

needles of sunlight
bouncing off bounce        of water
straight into the heart

## January 28

late winter in the northwest:

the eskimos have their 200 words for snow
i now have ten thousand words for grey

gull, cloud, water, mind
and so forth

## January 29

i curl into curl of shoreline sandstone
          into the ground of chuckanut earth
i open bare face to the sun, warming
          like a preening bird.
the placid wash of coruscate sea water on ears, brain.

i am given all this.
i give nothing of such substance back.

i look, listen, taste.
sit here.
and make this poem, these words.

it is what we do, our job.

## January 30

every morning now
watching
salmon seekers
ply the wet of dawn

          downriggers
                    —the cold lead ball,
                    cable slicing through
          mostly emptiness

## January 31

high tide, relentless west wind
crash, pounding of waves
shudders felt
all the way
inside the house

unsettling the ground
unnerving the center

## February 1

the hard edge of cold
seems gone for the year
green becomes greener

something stirs somewhere
with an almost-forgotten inkling
of resurrection

## February 2

the current islands of our western view,
the underpinnings of our visual lives:

clark, barnes, orcas
matia, sucia, patos
tip of waldron, bare, skipjack
pender, saturna
bits and pieces of other gulf islands
and beyond, the backdrop, the big one:
vancouver.

and almost,
missing only by about 30 feet or so:
alden bank

## February 3

the week's forecast:

rain turning to showers
cloudy with showers
clouds with occasional sunbreaks
clearing (but never quite clear)
partly cloudy (but no mention of sun!?)
intermittent rain and drizzle
steady interminable drowning downpours

add 3 jokers
reshuffle daily and print.

doesn't matter—
all have an equal chance
by tomorrow

## February 4

low low tide
beach drained, angled
out clean, down
to edge of sea lettuce and cobble

swept clear to the sky
looking kept and pure

i poke around, jealous
waiting
wanting the same treatment,
the same cleansing tide

## February 5

to move through
this life
in balance

i must
ground
to infinity

the cords here:
    into space—
        those rare days of spinning crazy cerulean sky
        those rare nights of scattershot light-pricks in the
    vastness of black

    and up the strait—
        that slightly tweaked
        horizon of flatwater

        no land, nothing beyond

        pulling me
        on
        and on.

planting me
    here
    now.

## February 6

wavesound (aloud, repeated until you get it right)

sh-yha. sh-yha.
shhhh-yha. shh-YHA.
shhhhhhh-yha. sh-yha.
shhhh-yha HURGH! SHHHH-YHA HURGH!
shhhh-yha. shh-yha.
sh-yha. sh-yha.

## February 7

moon

sure i know
it's cold, hard
mathematically scarred
white dust

but in this pre-morning
quivering and quavering
out of round
wobbling through cloud-skins

it stirs the unconscious
of creatures awake,
alive

## February 8

light posts of our night:

constellation of ski basins above
thin glimmer of vancouver below

point roberts floating
marooned in the void

navigational buoys, blinking blinking
strewn over the black wet unknown

red wink of mt constitution towers
ghostly phosphorescent yard light

all of this
shining at the tiniest center
of an infinite universe
of fleeing stars

## February 9

photons flung from sun
ricocheted off moon
scattered and crazed
on roil of night-water
straight through my eye

illuminating
my winter-dark
mind

## February 10

way back in the woods
in the center of a tall grass meadow
ramshackle shack
long abandoned
rusted stove, ratted mattress

each time i am here

i see
the ghost of brautigan
slouched in the doorway, funny hat
chewing on a pink chunk
of watermelon sugar

## February 11

dawn
full moon
sinking straight
into sucia

lighted clouds with perfect tight edges

i get the good
camera, tripod
ready, yes

moon drowns
in cloudbank
gone forever

## February 12

hard wind down
hale passage

ferry bobs

spits salt spray
on every windshield

## February 13

at the edge:
rock/water
urban/rural
dark/light
us/canada
continent/ocean
earth/space
life/death

in the center

## February 14

the steep downslope to the beach:

jumble and clash
of grappling greenery

wrestling roots
entwined tendrils

cedar and fir monoliths
anchoring all

slowly slipping
sliding sure-footedly

to the sea

## 15 February

each day
methodical, patient
sportfishermen work off our beach
searching for blackmouth

working on my mind
my instincts

catching
my fish
your fish
their fish

but mostly
no fish

## February 16

this night:
    stars strewn far across infinity
    full limpid moon
    the water emptied at low tide
    diaphanous milky light

    sharp black shadows
    of ancient firs
    daggering across
    glittering beach

so precise, so exact
and each glance, each breath
forges
an eidetic memory
deep in the mind
for eternal recall

## February 17

why is it
i cannot
often feel
and never
express
the arcane sum total
of experience—          beyond cause/effect
beyond noun/verb
beyond form/pattern
beyond synchronicity
beyond systems theory

but more numinous     graceful
poetic                    musical
than chaos,     just craziness
run amuck with protoplasm

is it only
because
there cannot be          we all secretly seek then —
a word for it?          knowing it, there is nothing
left to do, but pass away
to the next
unknowing as the wind

## February 18

first time this year
i get the boat
on the water

feeling that freedom
that elemental drive
to wander and explore, to harvest
from nature and its wild wet ground

the heft of the crab pot
the sharp tugs of
a rockfish supper

the lack of anything
resembling
a salmon

## February 19

oops!
it snuck up on me

everywhere—buds and blossoms:
salmonberry, currant,
unknowns

robins, robins, robins

the warm must
of an early spring

## February 20

foraging
i bring back
one stem of each
bloomer and budder

plopped into vase
"bouquet"
nipped for art, love
kept from their real work

i pray
there will be no reciprocity—
none of our more beguiling parts
plucked, displayed in some thicket

## February 21

a stone's throw away
the western horizon
a murky seamless void

hushed

## February 22

tiny and ethereal new leaves
fresh from our unseeable womb-spirit
pure, vibrant green

vivid as blood

## February 23

chopped marching scumble of silvergrey
stretches to a long thin layer
of deathdark smudged leadengrey
out to the lighted thread of horizon

the hulk of matia
an intense scraped dark void in the lightscreen
leading to a drooping sky of
stacked and bulging mammarous pulses

over-filled, dripping
the wet of the vast
warm and far
pacific

## February 24

snow
drops down
on mt. constitution

fruit trees
give
a nervous glance

## February 25

cabbage, chard and frilly kale
slowly thriving through
the mild winter
in strong and vibrant
bursting green

cruciform restorative
for the winter weakness
of body, soul

## February 26

dark purple coil of cloud
above matte-silver electric spread
                                                            of stippled water:

storm brewing, orcas already wet,
sucia shivering

## February 27

clear cut

*there was something here*

intact          integral
binding         held

a slow dynamic of exchange
beautifully performed

then a piecemeal studied obliteration
(like watching one's children
felled before one's eyes)

leaving only
ruts, shatter, debris
(like going home and finding
rubble, severed body parts)

*and now it is gone, trucked away.*

## February 28

out there
boat suspended in silver void
mirror line of grey horizon     under
powdered remnant of distant storm

and on our cluttered shore
pigeon perched on antenna
feeling pulse of oprah, rosie
our strange world, in here

## March 1

pitchfork
goat manure/barn straw
into truck

cart up to garden
spread, fluff
bless the ground

in the rain, of course.

## March 2

i glean a heart
shaped stone from
the beach streaked
and wrought with
geologic genesis

a four billion year project
of alchemy, patience, intentless
intent

just like us

## March 3

the color of water:

with wind
without wind

with sun
without sun

crepuscular
mid-day

in a glass
in a sea

## March 4

and some days
it smells a dry hard blue
hovering in a far horizon

and others
it smells a moldering green glop
oozing damply to inner lungs

but to touch
it feels the same
always different

like thrusting your hand
into your own blood.

## March 5

rearranging geology

walking the beach at low tide
find the perfect
weighted stone
fling it hard

wow!
skips and gambols
across three successive tongues
of 100 million year old
chuckanut sandstone
then flips and dives
zipping into the cold water

finding its new home
for the next thousand years
or so.

## March 6

half moon
reflected
off surface
of yard's tiny
rockstrewn pond

blinding the one
last goldfish

## March 7

cats creep, hunt
in heavy frost
of pre-dawn

lawn becomes littered
with carcasses
of songbirds, voles

meanwhile
i stalk and stockpile
the fish visions of summer

## March 8

we
and the world out there
and the world in here

    the twittering sparrow
    the color of the sky
    the heft of the planet
    the uttering      the weaving
    of words, dreams, agony, rapture

this moment:

    the complete
    presented history
    of the universe

## March 9

i go to the beach to watch time.

i see it coming
the twentieth wave out
but "by the time"
i see it

it has already
passed

## March 10

all i know for sure
is that
it has moved.

unless, of course
it is the center
and all else has moved.

## March 11

all right, closer.

nose to the shore/water interface.
wave splashes my face
this is now.

but by the time
i have thought it,
it has passed.

(time may not exist)
(time may be irrelevant)
(time does not read books)

perhaps it is only
sequence (if described)
flow (if experienced)

## March 12

truth is
i have gone
to the beach
to kill
time

## March 13

plum tree pops
puffs of white
first  to spring
in the tiny
orchard

## March 14

launch the skiff:

perky in the light slap of water,
the ten horse just right

but when empty tug rips past
throwing four-foot breaking wake

we (perkily) race to shore.

## March 15

the cacophonous rant
the blither
of urgent, importune frogs:

islands of crazed sound
in the night myst

## March 16

two eagles
clutch
to hovering scrag

eyeing
everything

## March 17

whipped wet

        rollers in the passage
        out into an infinity beyond
        pt migley buoy

        new coppergreen pilings
                stalwart and industrial
                never flinch
        ferry crew
                in shiny yellow suits
                moves curtly

directing with
warm, watery eyes

## March 18

that lovely warm
home of dusk
with its
spent energy
            hovering
            caressing

the last scattered cries
of day creatures

the first scattered cries
of night creatures

nuzzling

in arabesque
of sound

## March 19

marauding coons
every night
fondle and search
the pond rocks

wreaking havoc
with my zen rockscape

missing every time
the one fat carryover
goldfish

## March 20

first garden seeds
dry tiny flakes
but somewhere deep within
a stubborn germ
readies to grab
cosmic chemicals

and turn them into

arugula
broccoli
chard
escarole
lettuce
radishes

us

## March 21

cat and i
sit on lawn rocks
“glacial erratics”
watching last light leave

robin hurtles toward us
cat springs
four feet into air

claws deep
into robin’s past path—
just a tad late.

if i had half that quickness
half that instinct
fish would be stacked in the freezer
like cordwood

## March 22

neat tiers of books
huge flocks of words
captured and corralled
in such a way
that you begin to think
nature
is understandable.

but step out the door.
words do not flit through the air
words do not squirt through the ground
things and non-things slither and pulse
neither directed nor truly described
by our most perfect sentences.
the best we can do: just touch, wonder

and keep writing

## March 23

young slugs everywhere
so slimy, voracious

i try to squash them
and they squirt out

unharmed,
giggling

## March 24

bruised ragged light
held in wet lavender banks
rolling in from the deep

pulses of sun, tide
mystery

## March 25

embedded hulk of weathered megatrunk
on the beach, anchored
in some forgotten massive storm
must be doug fir, or cedar—big wood

i count 845 rings
remaining
there were more
—more than ten lifetimes

high tides slap inanely against its base
a million gulls have cruised past, a billion salmon
and we have sawed and hacked and picnicked
and perhaps felled it, built with its other parts

i nestle into its cut
the rings etched, warm
i move into its depth, length
like spring sap

it bears no grudge
and holds patience
            almost like a rock

## March 26

dusting of snow on orcas last night
rude welcome
for eight tiny goldfish
purchased to prey
on the flap-jerk mosquito larvae
in our narrow crack of a pond

## March 27

grilled the last fish in the freezer
august sockeye from legoe bay

rose pink flesh full of oil—
fuel for the long journey never made

i carry the carcass down
return it to the sea                    where

it will travel to crabs, gulls, dogfish,
and the tiniest of critters, plankton,

and, eventually, other sockeye.
passing through, into.        becoming.

just like us.
just like it has always been.

## March 28

sunset
ribbed vee
of flesh clouds

the framework of a fish
arcing through, filling
the dimming sky

encircling, keeping
feeding
this island world

## March 29

fine yellow
smokes out from limbs, blossoms
dusts the deck

in search of sex

            and nasal aggravation

## March 30

in the long run

(i don't care what
the biometricians,
the chaos theorists, the columnists,
the politicians, the corporate industrialists,
and all the rest of them funny off-islanders
say)

we are all one

## March 31

white shaft
of almost painful light
finds naval hole
in greyviolet gibbous
cloud mass

splays, explodes
on far water
blinding
blinding

blessing.

## April 1

i begin

to watch more carefully
for blips on the surface

to listen with purpose
for that exhaustive whoosh

i stay

somewhat on edge
waiting the return

of the felt power, the wild
the unknown vastness

of *orcas*

## April 2

blue
laid out flat
clear to the horizon
stippled and metallic

reflected into
the infinite
eggshell
of sky

telling
watery stories
for millions of light years
out there

## April 3

oily wriggling squiggles
in 3 AM look through the scope

moonbeams dance on calm waters
yellow or blue     almost nervous

almost like brain waves
of our deep sleep

unaware          alone
but still          vibrant, squiggling

## April 4

trash day

come late, jump in truck
wind tousled introductions
bright sun glare green whips past

we stop, team up
glean the ditches
for whisps of paper
cold aluminum
the ubiquitous styro peanuts
(use popcorn instead!)

"it's pretty clean this year"

fire station to legoe bay
bud and anna and dave and john
carole and i
listen to history, gossip, greetings
but over all, through everything

a harmony of trust

and rewards bestowed by
the jolly garbage queen
laughing, clapping
all of us
together
spreading back out
to our home

*for Lynn Day*

## April 5

beach fire

everyone has left
carole shoveling
redeyed coals and gravel
into the quenching sea salt:
hiss, white steam, white stars
black water
and gone

good night

## April 6

more garden:
saladstuff, peas, spinach
cold dirt under fingernails
concatenations of age
in my muscles, back

thinking about robbers and thieves:
deer, coons, pigeons, slugs.

## April 7

moon
night
beach
mirrorflat water
only the gentlest lap of wave

reflection of orcas
across the water:
shimmering, stately
leaping, chattering
chasing the hapless
ghosts of salmon past

## April 8

post-slack
the current slowly organizes
its confusion
its deadened inertia

wind flirts the surface
blowing opposite, teases
the unending, giggling
froth of desire

## April 9

we pry the skiff three hours
into the bounce and slap
of stiff cold wind

blackmouth search:
ghost fish on the screen
but the baits roll through
untouched

we beach to collect crab gear
glance back
ecstatically aghast—
there! massive arc
of barnacled grey whale

a hundred yards out, dives

never reappears, except
in our wild stories, wild memories

## April 10

the junk barges going north
with a season of supplies:
            trailers, boats, backhoes
            mystery containers
            stacked askew, perched
            seemingly ready to topple
plow through our little sea
practicing for the big stuff.

it is curious.
they never come back.

## April 11

frog croaking
creates a thousand seams
in the nightblack stillness

fills the voids
with lunatic cries,
incessant lust

## April 12

jigging at 280 feet
on the far waters
the surface a slapping confused chop
inky boat-swirling eddies
but below
in the calm
lines straight down
hefty goggle-eyed
tasty
rockfish

## April 13

i mow the scattered lawn
third time this year
inwardly complaining

but two cuts behind my neat-cropped neighbor

it should all be garden, flowers
tangle of salal, oceanspray, kinnickinnick
a wild and criminal campaign of weeds

## April 14

the water view:
clear turquoise sky
pure white sun
deep turquoise water

piercing skeins
of brilliant flatness
spiderwebbed with
riffles and rips

gulls and migrants
diving through the cracks
squealing, flitting
in ecstasy, orgasm

we may never
know
or fear
to allow

## April 15

men's lunch
at the beach store cafe

we talk of
floating strobed dancers
hermes' law
micromechanical somethings
smaller than a cell
the three tenets of inner peace
yurts

and why they took
tofu taco salad
off the menu

*for Kevin Jones*

## April 16

el niño

the rest of the world suffers
storms, drought, flood, famine.
we get
sunshine, a long
string of blinding bright days
and whisper warm nights

## April 17

lap of wave
darkening earth
turning from
engorging sun

it has
happened
this way
forever

## April 18

lap of wave
salmon sun floating
down into purple gulf islands
no clouds, the
light a seamless
transition from
fire to ash

all caught
in murky haze:
dust from china

## April 19

the water tonight is a being
a spirit
casting a spell
pulling from me
a heartened light
of excitement, fear

## April 20

i want to be out there
on a wet slab of wood
swirling in the tide mix
the wind chop, feeling

the pull of the moon
                                the mountain-islands
                                the farthest star
                                                of the last gleaming galaxy

## April 21

yes, the water is a being, a spirit
the same as
                    unending swells of
                    wind-whipped tall-grass prairie
                    the breath of peaks, snow-laced valleys

places without artifact
experiences without name
holders of *presence*

bathing my very tired        preoccupations
in lap of wave

## April 22

and i am held in the thought            lap of wave
that after us                            lap of wave
it will still be this way                lap of wave
forever.                                 lap of wave

## April 23

i toss beach gravel
back and forth      in my hands
back and forth
meditating.
watching.
waiting.

listening to the sound
of the tiny clattering rocks     against
lap of wave.

## April 24

the days of this spring:
blueful suspended light
warmth seeping into the winter earth
sprouting, bursting
green entangling sweet smells

and the nights.
the squealing, squirming nights!

## April 25

by warm soft night
they curl and creep
through open-window dreams,
and in the broad daylight
brazenly charge
our helpless architecture
and shrinking trails

underground, overhead
blackberry battles

bloodstab thorns
strangling stems

we hack and clip
knowing deep
that when we die
they will cover our graves
pry into the coffins
and make sweet fruit
from our best and worst

## April 26

minus tide
day-long sunbreak
people meander      dawdle
amongst tidepools, life

## April 27

the silvered surface of water
troweled and polished
flat      serene
in grey vacuum

suddenly shattered
startling black and white
frothy explosion:
hurtling male *orca*!

## April 28

latticed orbs
of slug-sweet dandelions
fuzzy puffs of translucent snowstorm
on all our banks, borders

our neighbors' neat-green
carries no such profusion
and we dutifully
clip snip and pull

in this fruitless war

## April 29

bald eagle sweeps through trees, across road
sweeps through mind
across plans:
new morning
of wing, wild eye

## April 30

the old second growth
of firs and cedars
roil and scatter, orchestrate
the restless
oceans of air
passing through, over
this island

never to be
the same

## May 1

mayday ceremony:
chants, bells, drums
music, prayers

new age old hippies and SwilKanim
wafting violin compositions
mesmerizing us on ground
his ancestors for twenty centuries
made totems and potlatches:

he calls

            the eagle

                        comes

## May 2

trusted
          like glass, good glass

the clarity, the invitation, of air
the why of water
patience of slow fire
crystal bond of earth

the once-shattered

          fused:

vitreous visions

*for Art Hohl*

## May 3

what has grown
into a basic need:

a vista, to a far horizon
with no trace of artifact—just "nature"

looking about the same
for a thousand years, ten thousand years

day after day
season after season

and at one point, far back,
never seen by man

## May 4

things hang, suspended
float instead of move
in milky emulsion

far out a wandering rip:
twirling and idling
through a viscous skin

of sea

## May 5

snarl of wingtip
hawk drops

rodent becomes
feather, talon

flight

## May 6

salmon season shut
sportboats gone

without boats, the water becomes

stark, wilder
vast
frightening, alluring

like the surface of the moon
like looking at new and wild country
for the first time

leading to the edge
of nothingness, of an
unspeakable and secret

need

## May 7

travel through
overgrown path

ward off
        blackberry
brush knee
        against tall grass

white blossomed branch
        of thimbleberry
spreads its wings

part the wild
        ocean spray's mane
the single whip
        of drooping alder branch

suspended from heaven
rooted in earth

*for Art Baner*

## May 8

looks like
this world
will be inherited by

slugs and dandelions
dogfish and starlings
nettle, blackberry

scotch broom

and the other
restless results of our
mindlessness.

## May 9

mile upon mile
of four billion year old saltwater
smeared smooth by no wind
ironed out flat
this day
in
slicked silvers
and glints of glimmer
and ghost clouds
        way off, rolled up
        over the islands, peaks
all in pale blue
vapor

## May 10

the damp seething

        shadowy sky in wet swirls
        purple blots and grey daubs
        smelling of iris and fir, roses
        and new ferns, all dripping

of this sunless life

## May 11

marking time through a windless calm
a steady swell kerfs neatly into the beach gravel

nothing out there to generate such:

perhaps
          ghost ships, far away, tracing endless wakes
          the pulse of gravity
          or the earth,

                    tossing in its sleep

## May 12

behind my house
wild maelstrom of tangle
looming ragged firs
harboring the nightcreatures

we go there to dream
of the sacred, the profound

and in the morning
we pray in the ether
that has seeped out in the night
curled around the houses,
flooded through our things.

no one touches this place.
we hold it in our breath.

## May 13

under, in the ground:

turgid roots and worming worms
swimming and swirling
in the slow damp current
of the depthless earth

and above, exposed:

the tidal creep of blackberry
the surf of thimbleberry blossoms
the sharp spray of scotch broom
spitting droplets of rufus hummingbird
far into the sky

## May 14

whatcom chief gone for two weeks of annual maintenance
we ride the 'squito, a 50 passenger foot ferry
out of our car shells, we meet, chatter on the crossing

hard wind, rain—december weather someone complains
the 'squito bounces at the dock, the old man next to me
says if he didn't have to feed his dog, he would have stayed
on the mainland, rented a hotel room.

do you ever get used to this weather—
how long have you been on the island?

he thinks, calculating.
over 70 years, and hell no.

## May 15

i watch the tai chi master
lock into qigong—
fluid, perfect movement

shaped yet unshaped

the same as
porpoise slipping through waves
(thoughtless/mindful silk in wind)

—the flesh of that energy

recognized
from waters barely, deeply

remembered

## May 16

puddles on pavement
reflecting perfect tree and sky

earthworm stretches across
the wet road, dodging traffic (!)

lummi mt shrouded in ominous cloud
opaque showers blur parts of outer islands

air tastes alive, tart
just like barely ripe salmonberry

## May 17

hunched raccoon on back lawn
i charge, clap, yell
it scampers back
to blackberry shelter

cats leap from hiding
arched backs     tails swollen, erect
give short and false chase
of skin-deep bravado

## May 18

sometimes, rarely, i see them first
the black slice of dorsal
arcing powerfully through the surface

but more often it is by sound:
the whoosh of their blow
        from a half mile away
the ring of craig's phone call—whales!
or the circus oohs and ahs
from off the weekend decks

## May 19

around in the passage
we bait with last summer's ling heads
drop the rings
drift off.

15 minutes        or half a beer
quick hoist, lurch over
and spiny crabs
scuttling everywhere

females and smaller males
plucked overboard
big males in the bucket
they will die, be eaten

and we will live, in grand fashion

## May 20

big slug slimes up, across
the kitchen glass door

it must feel like
walking on water or

            floating away, suspended in light

## May 21

show me the wind.
it is surely there, here

after all, we have a word for it.

## May 22

waves whip and slather
the grasses quiver
gulls soar, then are swept away

but where is the wind?

## May 23

the wind is here.
but where did it begin?

> the tiny freshet leaking from a snow bank
> that starts a river—
> and its tail
> the heavy and slowed current as the river
> stacks up against the deep ocean—

no—wind is different

without beginning, without end
the swirling soup that connects *everything*
invisible, delicate and subtle
holding deadly force

could we have not called it
god, tao, buddha?

## May 24

the first squirm of life
was blown about
by wind that was
already ancient

## May 25

wind
is just
a faster
less substantial
rock

## May 26

cold and dripping grey

craig gathers clams
the garden arrests
the slugs manifest,

        oozing everywhere

## May 27

first weekend of halibut season
flat tides all day
perfect water

brine the horse herring
collect the heavy gear
prime the vision of outer hein bank

up at 4:30, checking marine weather
"small craft advisory"
sustained 27 knot wind at smith island

i wander about all day
landlocked
aimless

## May 28

the expanse

of summer

space and

time stretch

every entity farther

but lovelier

## May 29

what blooms:

the painful yellow of scotch broom
weighted to the ground

the delicate robust white of cow parsnip
weighted to the sky

## May 30

in the sweet dawn smell
I stretch on rubber gloves
pour half a beer into a pail
and wander the terraces
of the lawn/garden

plopping slimy slugs
into a drunken death,
freeing their creeping souls
to an assuredly
higher reincarnation

## May 31

we bottomfish
from pt roberts
to alden bank
to matia
to clark
to sinclair
jigging hard

a dozen sea cucumbers
accidentally snagged
half a dozen dogfish
one nice cabezon
and no halibut.
no rockfish.
no lings.

these fertile waters
wiped clean.

## June 1

breathless sunset of
oily pink, salmon, violet
interlaced, floating
glowing, fading
transforming
light to matter to heart

## June 2

greenery
bulges pops spreads creeps explodes
swallowing trails and roads and houses
and maybe even
the slower-moving
creatures

## June 3

reach and pull
ripping
ripe waving grasses, spent dandelions
various and unknown forbs, herbs
“weeds”      in overspilling cartloads

exposing the chosen ivy, salal
various and known “ornamentals”
cultivated
by the small ordered visions
of our narrowed minds

and in another country
someone meticulously
culling what i save
coddling what i pull

## June 4

sunset mauve wash
hovering

within water/sky

within mind/heart

another spattering
in the mosaic
of experience, memory

hovering

## June 5

linen white thimbleberry
blossoms in dense scatter

robust and masculine
throbbing cow parsnip

skunk cabbage leaves like hammered
plates of thin green copper

all seducing, birthing, growing, multiplying
all springing from death
all summering toward death
in myriad singular beauty

## June 6

bulbous and fiery
orange sun
hissing
into far water

## June 7

three container barges
ponderous blocks of bulk
glacial movement against stiff tide

three canadian geese
in a single glimpse
bobbing in bronze reflection

walking mind
searches for connection
not seeing it is me

three blacktail deer
wary, diminutive, so vulnerable
to our presence.

## June 8

intentionless
pulse of wave
time after time
tongues the stones
shiny wet

## June 9

seven serpentine otters
slithering through the sunset
just off shore
curious and wary
silent as shadows

## June 10

drone of tugs
dark hulk of barges
against the tide
muscling through
soft apricot sunset

suspended, kept
in breathless pastel

## June 11

hard west wind
all night we hear
the cough of waves
on the shore

and at dawn:
eagles, ravens, gulls
cruise the surf line
eyeing the upheaval

for sustenance

## June 12

carole takes the walk through the woods
brings me news and 6 ripe salmonberries

ocean spray and blackberries blooming
blood red elderberries

ferns to six feet!

## June 13

dawn and
6 *orcas* offshore
baby chortling straight up
cavorting the choppy surface
reveling in the early light

## June 14

i walk the road at sunset
raccoon with her two babies
foraging the roadside
barely cares
i am close

## June 15

scrumbling through sea rocks
wedged in centuries of shell shards
lurking slimy and spined
critters of the muck
and the odd steamer
            popped in the bucket

the clam scent
almost like sex
into our fingers
and later
down our tongues

## June 16

walking home late
through tunnel of grey shrinking light
too easily wandering
into the nether parts of night
and its dark tendrils
of fear and trust
succor and risk

## June 17

we are this way:

gleaning the beach for sculpted stones
pocketing some                most go back
"need more work"

                                   maybe a thousand years
                                   maybe ten thousand years

                  then someone can say
                  it's ready, finished

and place with the others
with fossils and shards and shells
on our window sills:

hardened prayers, icons.

## June 18

that infinite instant
of eye contact—
blackeyed blacktail
antlers in velvet
inflating with blood and

the coming urge to mate

and later
the velvet touch
of thimbleberry leaf
nuzzling the back
of my slow hand

## June 19

double rainbow
arc'd prism of every color
replicated, placed
just so, in resonance

the infinite play
of infinite energy

## June 20

we bike the woods
spatter and squirt down
the mudslime path

gliding through
sun/greenshade cool

the soft erotic brush
of thimbleberry on our hands
laced with the long sting
                                        of nettle.

## June 21

cool cloudy and breezy solstice
longest day, shortest night
and tomorrow until mid-winter
days grow shorter

summer lags though,
still wresting the sky
from the scudding wet
pulses of spring storms

## June 22

the galumph of emergent sun
charges our focus          the eye-shattering green
we gorge on light, wallow in warm
drop clothes, open the windows
of winter's containment

## June 23

some part of my body
some mysterious alchemic
          current of physiology
binding strength, protection
comes from her

many months ago
pricking cold soil with
smooth pearly-hard cloves
waiting, knowing through winter
watching the pale curl of sprouts
snipping out the slugs each morning
patient
then pulling, sorting, cleaning
bagging, braiding, powdering

offering as garlic
every farmer's market
until we are all stocked
and well

*for Nancy Simmerman*

## June 24

sun flattens
pulled taut on horizon
centered up georgia strait
          just shy of texada

the earth pulls away
powdered rouge of sky shrinks
and the waters follow, reluctantly

          caressing and streaming

          as if leaving a lover
          for the last time

## June 25

black hole of night
and the blackberry blossoms
like clusters of galaxies
suspended, floating out there

ghost sun white of petals
star burst of anthers
and deep within moon of ovary:
grain of sand

## June 26

mid-afternoon

one of those days
          turgid, augury
when i could
          reach out, touch
the farthest islands
that wisp of cloud

## June 27

the sea floats on the earth
the sky floats on the sea

i am caught between, within

the thick fluid of water, blood
the thin fluid of air, thought

floating, barely
breathing

it hardly seems
necessary

## June 28

hottest day of the year thus far
might have hit 80
sticky, hot, been in town

lummi kids
splatter in water
off the ferry dock

i go to the beach
to wade, to cool
my soft winter feet
prickled and tickled by the gravel

aaugh!
cold water aches to the bone
travels up, clasps my heart in hard grip
i back out, yelping

## June 29

in winter
things are close, insular
dark.
i meditate, write.
introvert.

but summer

stretches far beyond my reach
boundaries evaporating in evanescent shimmers of light.
i just want to move, touch, do.
with no thought, no reason
no prayer.

## June 30

shoulder-high grass
heavy heads hanging
to the marvelous blue-dazzle heavens

blackberries snaking below
scotch broom burgeoning
unto the sky

bordered by blossoms
of wild rose already tattered
unto the earth

the barely apparent
nod and twitter of long stems
from the not-apparent wind/spirit

## July 1

all day on the chop
off pt roberts
in search of salmon

half a dozen dogfish
a flounder for the grill
and nothing else

        but rolling purple wave
        pure white froth skittering
        into the open, infinite air

to breathe, to breathe

*for Tom Reardon*

## July 2

the fireworks stands
of the lummi reservation

in the tidal flood plain of the nooksack
    not that long ago
    a people of long houses
    long journeys in long boats
    trailed out to harvest
    and gather molluscs, fish and
    red meat from the freshwater land

now behind bright paint plywood shacks
named
    big thunder
    outrageous raymond's
    jack's bomb shack
    t & a explosives (now what does that mean?)
    and the best:
    granpa ernis firework

trading for white man's money
bartering, taking what
the land gives them

## July 3

deep evening
front moves in

clouds the color of slate
    water the color of clouds
        sky the color of water
            leaves the color of sky
                eyes the color of leaves

the color of slate
    the smell of slate
        the taste of slate
            the sound of slate

## July 4

on the beach, finally dark at 10:30
crowds scattered in beach fires:

popping vibrant colors of the deep cosmos:
explode, burst, spray,
detonate, shake, bang,
shatter, splash, splatter,
smoke, fizz, spume,
blast, bang, boom!

the oohs and ahhs
the rapture of erupture!

## July 5

sun down
in the darkness of firs
in the quiet of their wracked deadfall limbs
          the mangled power, holding

the now dim dual blossoms of twinflower
a few early and tart thimbleberries wiped into mouth
birds settle their chatter into night nests

and the air, wakening
          exactly
                    smells the taste of
                    cold pure spring water
          trickling clarity
into all, fresh

## July 6

hummingbird caught
in cat's claw clasp
i hurry out

but it has died
          except for its eyes

shiny black wet
still glistening
with deep tropical nights

## July 7

clouds stream, pour
out of orcas, splay
to the northeast, cast
overwhelming shadows
          and fill the entire sky, earth

everything we do seems small
thoughts seem furtive, and
are hidden away

i feel exposed, vulnerable
and slip into tree shade
knowing my part in this
is to merely
          bear witness
          to much larger
          energy

pouring.
streaming.

## July 8

the aeolian drifters—
spiders, gnats, the strong of wing
light of body
rise from the island
blow to the west on
upswirl of storm
alighting lightly on
speckling
the snow fields, the glaciers
on mt baker
          all the while we recieve
          immigrants from
          orcas and vancouver islands

## July 9

evening:

saucy stellars, cocky kingfishers
heron cranking slowly up the passage
          eagle at the snag on pt migley

strollers and bikers flood the roads
clamorous dinner at the café
          reefnet boats being set

last of strawberries, raspberries close
mock orange and white clover blooming
          all roots searching deeper, stronger

grasses heavy with seed, fields being mown
deer sleek and tame
          as are we

## July 10

wild-strewn cobble
of stones on the beach
placed      exactly
in the neatswept sand
by wave and wind

in perfect alignment      with

          every adjoining rock
          by color, by space, by size

          every planet, every star

          every thought, every hope
          all future, all past

an astrology of scatter

## July 11

this place
this day
is like mercury

held in the hand
shimmering, bulbous

a wobbling sphere
of reflected light

of barely contained
energy

## July 12

something not
of light, or sound
of flesh, or fiber

something to curl into
to suckle

to find,
nurture

## July 13

against the dark flanks
of sucia, so wild and desolate
in winter, white splashes
of canvas, hulls
stacked and gay

crowded in destination

## July 14

light from hidden sun
bounces off moon
bounces off water
bathes all in ivory light

blocked by the old firs
inky jagged silhouettes
shadowing across the
sterile white
immaculate beach

## July 15

what we don't see:

eagle drifts
folds, shrieks

eagle
drifts
folds
shrieks

eagle drifts
folds shrieks

dives toward
hapless prey
on the opposite
side of the earth

## July 16

something changes, shifts

it starts in the ferry line
—suspended—
the world behind, the island ahead
an exploration of the art of waiting

load into the womb-shaped ferry
fellow travelers, familiar guides
it is all liquid, whether light or dark
at the non-speed of water

landing, the deep smell
of open space, calm
houses subordinate to the land
the ever-tangled green.

and a culture simple enough to understand:
a store, a café, a post office.
a fire department.
enough.

it isn't only that
the pace is slower
it is also deeper
for each of us, in our own way

## July 17

at dusk
in the woods

i try to move
within the energy
of the place, of the trees

where my sound
belongs

where i don't intrude
frighten

where i am invited in
to the next space

i find
i cannot go
slowly enough

standing still
is too fast

i have to back up
            wait      —

*there.*

## July 18

wave curls into shore
thins, fills with light
becomes depthless translucent turquoise
filled with roiling energy and whirling twitching matter

the alchemic stew
eternally transmuting
water and salt and rock and light
to protoplasm, heart, mind

## July 19

it is in our memory
when there were no words

but experience seemed to sometimes coalesce
into meaning, some sort of bewitching unity

which gave forth—birthed—words
and each word was a poem—marvelous, infinite

blossoming to a litter of words, sentences, stories
books and thoughts
of every unimaginable sort

and now:
there is something here
—many somethings—
sure, strong, active
for which there are no words

i cannot tell you

look.
breathe.
apprehend.

remember.

## July 20

the piquant green
drains into darkness

murmuring

## July 21

young vine maple

nurtured in dark supple shade
ten floating leaves
absolutely flat, absolutely parallel
                                                    to the earth

the trunk merely a stem
a thin drawn wire
that bobs and swirls

at a mere breath

## July 22

some visitors
wander uncomfortably
confused, unsure
on the beach                    having forgotten

others
seep in
excited, eyes vibrant as light
swirl the sand
gather stones
say "boat" and "gull" and "wave"

touch the water
laugh in rhythm

## July 23

rock at tideline
in perfect formed shape of itself

striated and smooth and dark
crystalline interstitial lattice
shifted and tumbled by waves

a billion times

placed, ground amongst other rocks
larger and smaller
until each one fits

it is here, in this place, exactly
because of all that.

perhaps there should be an understanding
prayer     reverence     agreement

if it is picked up     pulled out
flung far away     or taken home

## July 24

the vast of deep summer
        the lazy waft of heron
        rolling swells of dry flaxen field grass
        the sweet chill air of dawn/dusk
        leaves luxuriating under strong full sun

                and the horizon stretches
                beyond the edge of the earth

                and the sky is not a bowl
                but an expanse of warm infinity

## July 25

there is no up
there is no down

only toward the center
and away from the center

and the center is chosen.
it is an understanding with gravity.

and directions—north, south, east, west
    just circle and circle
    endlessly

the only meaningful travel:
    toward the sun
    away from the sun

## July 26

where can i hold
in the center of stillness?

the three directions:
we revolve about an axis, spinning
circling the wandering sun in light and dark
all floating, curving through space

tides pulse back and forth
the marine plate grinds into the continent
the winds swirl this way and that

and the center
of an infinite universe?

i can only push hands, stick
never hold, never truly stick

only be held
and carried.

perhaps in the vastness
between the hectic particles.

## July 27

not just watch (the tree bends, trills in the wind)

beyond being a part (i am here, the tree is there)
become, unite (we stand inside each other)
be (we are both blown by the same wind)

wrest the presence (we bend and breathe together)

—dance—

## July 28

night sculpins
fan the dark water
off the ferry dock

lit by the fluorescent light
of their heaven—
angels
                    tending their business

## July 29

on the beach, night
full moon, low tide
no clouds

the landscape a jumble of light and lesser light

senses awry—the world is
          black, lesser black, blacker
          glitter/non-glitter
          grey, grey holding more light, grey holding less light

some edges tight, precise
others scumbled, evanescent

the waves, enigmatic and profound
adamant pulses of light/dark

and i am here, there     reflected and scattered
anchored only by the aged contrails
                                                                  of fleeing stars

## July 30

a tiny pool of trapped water

nestled in smooth rock

reflecting a wobbling

distended oozing moon

## July 31

blustery blood sun
earth turning fast away
ragged tops of swept waves
dusting off into
the churn and furl of all

caravans of carved canoes
plying spanish galleons
lumbering russian fur-seekers
gillnetters, purse seiners
kayaks, sailboats

and the pilgrim from *on the beach* in his last act
trolling in his skiff, for the ghost salmon
just off shore

## August 1

raspberry
the color of
the taste of
the touch of

that tangy sweet
soft nipple

## August 2

the busy blinding mind of summer's sun
pull the weeds, cut the grass
battle the blackberries

host visitors, take vacations
work feverishly on last winter's list
of bright sky fantasies.

saving the poems
for the grey moody days
of winter

## August 3

this piece of water
is alive, likc us

breathing steadily through its electric surface
dreaming, lusting for the moon
seeking its path
sloughing off old cells along the shore

holding fish and other
wriggling, slimy, prickly
critters

just like our bodies nurture
a fecund garden
of bacteria, parasites

our blood saline as the sea of the sea
our minds memory holding

common fathomless

mystery

## August 4

three dead hummers in four days
our cats become expert

they hunt to hunt
not from hunger

our guilt—the luxury
of pets, the death
of free birds

robbing a mate, a nest,
a niche—what will pollinate now?

the big cycle:  the wary
will survive, reproduce

the cats will begin to miss
and pad home each night

to be fed.

## August 5

            softly wrinkled
oyster clouds
            smelling of slow and tender sex
serene corrugated shirr
            against grey rose void

                        suspending planets

                                    like pearls

## August 6

i take my glasses off
and try to shut down the words
to the point where

i don't know
if that tree will bite or burrow
or fly off into the greying cosmos

and then a clump
of thimbleberries
becomes a being      and invites me in

heart first

## August 7

a neatly-scribed rising
sun     in iridescent phase-change
moving through     electric-
mauve vaporizing clouds

the long languid days     of heat
finally catch up
to the winter chill
remnant in the deep earth

thick banks of recent water
drape over the islands and open sea
as if to suffocate
silhouettes

of herons at dawn
gleaning low tide shoreline
focussed, feeling pressed          by memory
of relentless cold rain          of dim winter days

    but by afternoon
    all will swelter
    fog burned off
    herons sated
    in the drowse of summer

## August 8

seed heads hang
bowing grass stems
back to the earth

berries ripen, find deep color,
roots swell, become reservoirs
all storing transmogrified photons

most of their works given as gifts
passing along their energy
to other forms

only a very few
chosen
to reproduce

it has always been this way

how could i
ever
be that generous?

## August 9

glacial erratics
plucked from the house excavation
four boulders
the size of large curled bodies
coupled bodies

each feels different

different
history
energy
presence

each unique holding strong

displaced

in concert

*for Gwen Schnurman*

## August 10

reef netters
perched like hungry herons
spring the nets
leap to their catch
flop fish into the hold
reset and reperch

peering hard
knowing these days, these fish
are numbered, and precious

## August 11

i perch on the edge of the island
in my starved heronmind
spring open to the water, sky, earth
leap to my poems
(flop words into the hold)
reset and reperch

peering hard
knowing my days, our days
are numbered, and precious

## August 12

the spirit of august is vacant     slack
    like a river entering a lake
    suddenly viscous, disjointed, ponderous
            waiting
    like a slow clotted eddy
    holding the scavengers, the gleaners

            (exactly like, when i was a kid catfishing
            in the hot night, the lantern, drooping lines
            the mosquitoes, rancid bait, the smell of milky mud)

a void to become lost in
to forget

to be lulled

## August 13

if you don't
touch, breathe
kiss in every way possible

you will only know
what you think
you know

## August 14

taste the air
breathe it deep into bone
exhale through toes, fingers

the taste
of primordial glop
death roar of dinosaur
incredulous gasp of the first word

shared by all living, all non-living
past, present, future.

taste!

## August 15

i lean into the tree
ground into its roots
suck sun and make air with its needles
feel its blood flow both ways
feel it flex in the breeze

feel it touch

me

## August 16

*an eskimo carver listens for the shape within the stone*

i walk the beach
pick up stones that look interesting—
        wet colors of blood, pearl, night, fire
        patterns of marbled wood, jupiter, nebulae

        but they are all smooth warm energy in my palms
                (who needs crystals?!)
        I hold them and walk

i hear no shape
i *hold* the shape

        they are done, complete.
        their stories are told, exactly

i toss them far out     plop, plop, plop
        thinking
                how many centuries before
                they're back to the beach

in new, still-completed shapes
telling
new stories

## August 17

frantic
        work at work
        mow the lawn
        cook dinner
        drink wine
        sit in the grass
        watch sunset
        become dark
        drift
        into the
        non-
        speed
        of this place
still

## August 18

jumpers

flee gravity in joyful leaps
exuberant silver shudder
comes through surface
into something that must feel
like nothingness

to knock off sea lice
to escape a seal
to get bearing

perhaps just
to take a look

## August 19

the blinding obscurity
of fog

the comfort of believing
there is nothing beyond

that we are held

## August 20

there is a strangeness
an unease
almost frantic, ethereal
felt, not seen—the portent of autumn

        the smell of shorter days
        the truths
                no longer languid
        come harder and faster
        as the death of summer
        is foretold in every stiffening stem

i am pulled          swirled          beguiled
swallowed and held
into its dense and dangerous

beauty

## August 21

gleaners:
	the gulls, the dogfish
	coyotes and coons
	thistle and nettle
	scotchbroom, slugs
	poets and potters

surely
the last		to go

## August 22

every morning
an hour or so before dawn
	before any light
	before any hint of change
the heron groans from its roost
behind the house in hideous screech

how does it know when it's time?
	(in heron-mind any time is perfect)
		heron-mind perhaps does not watch for change
		heron's flight *is* the change

the earth turns, the moon floats around
the heron squawks, then leaps

all the same

## August 23

the inland forest
jumble of growth
second growth, regrowth
crazed, wild   anarchic
limitless   tangled
and god-like growth

the spaces all of us come from
the places where no one goes

## August 24

the smell of blackberries—
    the deep of earth
    the must of sex
    the dark stain of its juice
    the burgeon of wild growth,

of reckless sun

## August 25

as it was told to me

    there would be a place
    in a meadow, near the forest edge,
    behind my house, beyond the road

    where it would be different
    there would be strength, energy
        dancing, vibrating

she said it would be like being beamed up

    it was, only i never left

## August 26

stalwart massive cedar
drooping branches
lattice of layered bark

rooting into the damp and pliant earth

i lay my hand onto the bark
to touch, to understand.
something opens. it moves far inside.

## August 27

evening
front stalled at far edge of sound
light on water looks
a weak yellow acid
prickled with
indeterminate wind, tide

is this the end of summer?
i am not sure.

porpoise breaks the surface
once
way out

never reappears

was it really there?
did it happen?
i am not sure.

and the yellow light
is now grey, purple, silver –
either the gentled warm of summer
or the uneasy foreboding of autumn

i am not sure

## August 28

no wind.
the bleary salt surface
slowly undulating

like a measured, sure orgasm

## August 29

i stand and watch.
eagle appears.

    one mind:
        i happen to be there
        eagle happens to be there

    the other mind:
        eagle appears
        because i am there

    the far mind:
        i appear
        because eagle is there

## August 30

two snakes
slithering rivulets of black blood
traceless like a dreamt ghost

it is the motion
the quick slickness of it
that draws the dread

## August 31

the vast coherency
is larger
than thought
larger than this island
larger than this universe.
but held, centered
on each piece of grit on the beach
each wisp of wind, each droplet of dew, each leaf, each breath.
but to say how it works—
"connected" "balanced" "a world of relationships" "pulsing rhythm"—

the words are so small, and tired

## September 1

rock becoming soil
becoming plant becoming
body becoming mind
becoming spirit becoming
mind becoming body
becoming plant becoming
soil becoming rock

fueled by light

nothingness becoming somethingness
becoming energy becoming
matter becoming awareness
becoming spirit becoming
awareness becoming matter
becoming energy becoming
somethingness becoming nothingness

fueled by god

each inhales
each other's exhale

each a different aspect of the same breath

## September 2

i sit in the meadow
            thinking
                        watching
                                    feeling
                                                joining
the coherent vastness
                                    grabbed by wonder

everything just
whirring and whizzing
15 billion year old molecules
of a loving cantankerous god

            was there a beginning?
            will there be an end?

            —only if you can stop/hold this instant

## September 3

a wiggling network, a web of humming strings
supported, fed and controlled,
by breath, touch, energy.
    presence.
"infused dynamic balance"

it is all about movement, change, transformation
(nothing, *nothing* is static)
                some in less than an instant
                some in billions of years
    objects are not objects
    they are this becoming that
    (objects only in the snapshot of our consciousness)

eating and being eaten
fueling and providing fuel
passing from one state of bliss to another
            (and we have the audacity to call this death?)
    from subatomic particle/wave
    to the imagined endlessness of the universe

and at the infinite center:
    immanent calm, knowing
    every act is sacred, perfect

## September 4

the irony of consciousness:
when we look, we think
and separate ourselves from the nature/spirit,
but only through thinking/looking
can we find our way back
to pure consciousness, unseparated
dancing in the vast coherency

    what is beyond cognitive sensation?
        (for starters, most of the electromagnetic spectrum)
    what is beyond our understanding?
        (direct apprehension)
        (things working without us)

## September 5

the existence and working of things
                        as they are

as we see them
think about them
describe them
organize them
                        as they are

                        floating in the divine

is there a thing?    vortex, concentration of intent    the seen
is there an event?    no, just continuous flow    and the
unseen

the grass bends to the wind
it moves, returns, but
it is not the same

## September 6

i walk with the beach
just waves, gulls, grit, grey—moving
coherent vastness

## September 7

coyote
scampers on this shore of primal wonder
feigns attack, howls
yaps insanely
tosses everything into the air—

o, the wondrous squealing and splashing!

## September 8

leaves on cherry tree
hang limp. spent
from hot light,
a season's work

of crimson swollen fruit
that fueled for a day that
raucous band of gypsy thief crows
now gone, marauding elsewhere

while the gentle deer
nuzzle the sweetening apples,
waiting
for their taste
of the hot light
in the coming
cold

## September 9

the expansive nest          (the lack of request)
the reverberating womb          (the lack of the unknown)
the resting fortress          (the lack of fear)

of

silence

## September 10

last light
waves wet sand in
silver serrated scallops

way out  a strange
greyghost bird, a shadow,
wends and wafts away

gone, forever unknown

## September 11

fraser river pinks
migrating along the island, teeming
upshore, downshore, at any instant
a dozen or more fish leaping into our world

in gathering darkness
i whip my rod toward the flurry
hook up on every cast, beach five
writhing feasts, hard, solid, strong
in rare requited lust

and eventually
arm aching, dark
the river of fish still surging
drag my catch up the hill

## September 12

predawn barely
apprehended forms:

a still sea of air
the color of void
a still hulk of water
the color of reflected void
the darkness of matia and orcas
more substantial by only a shade

perfect sphere of moon
a gaudyglitzy neon pumpkin

suspended in all,
in the sweet smell
of pure fall

## September 13

the thermometer reads the same
as days in august
but it is different

in the groin, in the heart

perhaps like marching into battle
the fear, the passion
the wild excitement
of storm. winter.

it is coming. i feel it.
i know. everything knows.

## September 14

sunset
a thin combed wisp
of cirrus
alive
burning with light

islands purple and black
the water marching north
under a tousling breeze

and above
nothing
except the odd molecule
between me
and the far edge of the universe

## September 15

spiders everywhere
*everywhere*
profusion, a lattice of webs
a congestion of sticky strands

the networks of a late harvest
the last chance
to entwine the careless
the fat, the naive

i walk with more caution

## September 16

water
shore
light

what have you imagined?
now close your eyes.
listen. . .

## September 17

it all depends on
        the clarity of water
        the frequency of waves
        the inclination of beach
        the mix of sand/gravel/rock
        the color of sky
        the angle of sun

        where i stand
        and other things
                which i cannot tell

                (such as the sound of color that day)

## September 18

loons everywhere
scribbling the signature of fall
on the flat flat water

## September 19

whisks of thin slate clouds
raspy ragged in last of sun
in a short glance as if
they were static, painted

but i remember
to open into some
          rhythm?          pulse?          other dimension?
a fuller view
          —like snowflakes through the windshield

and the clouds contort, swirl
          hypnotic, alive as mass, as aggregation
i hold back on the last edge
          unwilling, too sure (yet)
to be sucked
into something like
infinity
divine, seductive          infinity

## September 20

birds:
creatures that fly
(rats with wings)

          names
          get stuck, mired
          in details, commonness

birds:
beings of moving air
unfurled resplendent grace

and flight. . .     marvelous flight!

## September 21

hard nw wind and magnificent sun

full blast deep turquoise water and sky
sailboat carved from slices of a taut, white balloon
skitters on tight frothing chop

the island flexes, searching for better footing
the first yellow leaves swirl,
the old firs howl

the luff of the planet
as it is brought around
into the change of season

## September 22

clear night
                    white moon
reflected on
                    black water
that wobbly image
                    mirrored back to moon

          —sees itself!

as do stars
          some 4 thousand light years later!

## September 23

the thusness of the soil
works its way
up the trunk, the limbs
to the vast sky
in sprawled scatter
of gabbling, gleaning green
sucking sustenance
from sky, sun

and now, leaving the green
to the core truth
of falling reds and yellows
returns to its source
laying nourishment
for the next

the thusness of the water
squirts smolts of silver salmon
out in rivulet, down mainstem
to the vast sea
in sprawled scatter
of gobbling, gleaming feed
sucking sustenance
from sea, sun

and now, leaving the boundless
seeking the truth
of birthplace
returns to its source
to lay on redds
for the next

## September 24

winter augury

strange pregnant
lenticular clouds
too crisp in detail

holding with
hazy smear of
indeterminate fog

cats stay in the box
for the morning
in trance

midafternoon sun
vaporizes all
clouds have disappeared

but are not gone

## September 25

the chirp of crickets slows
now only an occasional croak of frogs
life hangs suspended
knowing
winter
births on every breath
gathers on every quiver

## September 26

chirp and trill of birds
merges
into my body, cells
changing, attuning
healing from each note

## September 27

two days of hard wind, hard blue skies
everything swirling, swirling
    tree blown down, power out for 6 hours
    two kayakers
    headed for patos from lummi
    drown, boats in pieces
    probably never made it past
    the wild standing chop off village point

then four days of large calm
bright skies bright stars

    like taking a photo of stillness
    and living within it, without breathing

## September 28

this morning
long before the sun
pleiades glittering
          in direct transmission to retina
          in full unconscious meaning

## September 29

absolute quiet.
no noise.
absolute
          silence of solitary sounds.

## September 30

haze like white powder
reefnetters float on the platforms
peering
for glints of reflected light
to bounce silver in their nets

## October 1

delicate neon filigree
trickling through
thick slate slab
of heavy cloud
oozing over vancouver island

last prayer of summer
caught within the first winter surge

## October 2

walk to beach
dip hand in water
dab the cold wet
to forehead

a collection of remnant molecules from
    the dark depths of rosario strait
    a skittering wave against slave trade canoe
    trickle off canyon creek
    glacier melt on mt baker
    rain off my roof
    condensate from troposphere

here, washing this beach

## October 3

that place
    where
i am moving with the earth
    in perfect synchronicity
circling the sun
    in slowspiral
flowing to the outer universe
    in harmonic vibration

with sun's rays on my skin
i dissolve, release
become my own heart's true beat
and cast no shadow

*for Barb Phair*

## October 4

like some unending horizontal waterfall
the vast west vibrant water
gripping crisp violet
streaked with deep turquoise riffs
strutting white caps, sharp

and the message is this:
    it is larger, more powerful
    than we can think

on days like this
places like this
we are merely
frail witnesses

## October 5

the garden a tumult of now-sagging overgrowth
gone wild like always

(i am a planter, not a maintainer)

deer and raccoons trample the corn
i salvage half-ears, nibbled away

dig potatoes, pluck beets
preen the bolted chard

pledging, like always, next summer
fewer poems, more hoeing

## October 6

four days of drizzle, grey, damp
dreary dimness
then cloudless blast
of electric blue sky
and almost painful light

i sit on the beach
and just stare at the sun

## October 7

i eat the summer
too-young ears of corn (already nibbled by deer)
blood vein leaves of chard (large, as tough as deer's ears)

feral potatoes grown from the seed missed in last year's harvest
(like this year's fawns, grown from does missed by last year's hunters)

i am glad to share my garden with the deer
and glad and grateful to eat their wild cousins from the far mountains

and glad to eat their left-behind ancestors
—ling, rockfish, cabezon
from the far waters

## October 8

skiff twirls in tide run
green candlefish jig
thirty feet deep off gooseberry point
wham! surge!
a play of perfect resistance,
wet net, flapping strong
seven pound silver salmon

## October 9

fleeing vortex of sun
sucking in last of summer like a black hole

leaving only the perennials

those of us who
can speak
with winter

## October 10

deep iceblue glaciers
hug and crumble the hardness
of mt baker, bleed cold milk
in summer, tumbling down
in grace of gravity and
ooze across the north county
flats into dendritic
stolen soil delta, dumping
murk into the ancient yielding
brine of the sound, circling
flanks of lummi island like a
deep iceblue glacier

## October 11

the air reeks and snaps
    of fermented windfall
    brittle bright leaves
    the last lovely and soft sun of the year—
        i smell
            the plunder of summer's work
            the bare stem of winter
            the last breath of warm play—

                each breath, at once

## October 12

through a window

| line of sky | depthless blue | infinite as we know it |
|---|---|---|
| smearwisp of cloud | white stroked grey | ghostly dimensional |
| line of sky | bleached yellowblue | warping away, wrapping back |
| streak of far island | milky blue | the draw and lust of distance |
| streak of near island | greypurple | i touch, and stand connected |
| line of water | metallic cleft, black | an entire world, hidden |

the sun is such a complex god

## October 13

swirling mosaic of leaves
crimson spotted yellow
fat salmon and lambs, bled and gutted for winter stew
curled essential bronze browns
so true it roots restless flight right back into the earth
and painful lustful reds
drawing blood to the throat, hearts to the sky
all under the naked blue of the very very precious last days

tossed and tossed into the air by the sooth-saying winds
until they finally fall in exact accordance
with the way it will be

## October 14

rugged slamming nw wind
rollers pounding the beach
the sound of crushing
summer's growth of
seaweed, plowed into
the sand, compost

## October 15

old ragged fir on the point, steadfast and solid
has no boundaries, never ends:

anchored to the earth
held up by the earth

roots commingling with slather of microbes and wandering worms
incessantly probing the dark soil, farther, farther

gases of the air spewing back and forth through its needles
sending stray molecules of fir out on the winds, forever

suspended by the sky
pulled up by the sun

more present and more precarious
more like a rock and more like a memory, every year

## October 16

i come from the desert southwest
and understand:

wet as miracle
every drop a blessing

## October 17

the days shorten
but the nights lengthen
to sleep and dream
to restore the fatigue of enlightenment
in the fecund nether-womb of endarken-
ment

## October 18

fourteen thousand years ago
mile thick glaciers
hauling granite boulders
from far b.c. mountains

smearing, compressing
these islands
then melting, vaporizing

leaving the boulders
—erratics—
as clues
reminders, gifts

## October 19

fog blind:

you remember

to listen.

to imagine.

## October 20

solitary flirting gust of wind
etches nest of black prickles on the water

directly above
a pastiche of dark/light birds

wavers, feigns, darts, swirls

twining, dancing
the nexus of one mind

## October 21

big leaf maple leaves discordant mix of color
draped, stacked over sharp quarry-blast roadbed
like a gaggle of starfish gorging on our leavings

## October 22

dappled blacktail buck
antlers curved symmetry of tines
rigid and polished in maleness
swollen neck, head down, scenting

back of my neck
primeval skin/hair/flesh
prickles, rises, heats

## October 23

are these rocks my body?
did i come out of this salty water?
did i make this air, or did it make me?
and why, o god, why
explain
this stunning beauty

## October 24

hundreds of bobbing gulls
collected, gathered
gabbling

on the barely undulant sea
in perhaps the last of open sun
for months

raucous, impudent
in the evanescent
stillness

## October 25

besieged by the turmoil of autumn

constellations of snowberries
                    hung for winter
a few renegade blackberries
                    still blooming
brownish moonscape of mushroom
                    gills as cold as trout
the lonely creak of chickadees
                    against the silence of the migrants

i tumble in the landscape
like a leaf in a tinkling stream
until i descend into the shore of the sound
profoundly hazy, still:

it is almost too much.
i touch the water to my forehead.
it is cold and pure as a stream—
                                        that tinkling stream

## October 26

remnant leaves on the chokecherry thicket
in spattered patter
of sinusoidal wave        (like tiny determined butterflies of sun)
the last color of summer
perched for its last littering flight

## October 27

big leaf maple leaf
floats down into
swarm of thimbleberry leaves
bringing news, stories
from far above

## October 28

the tickling prickle of fir needles
the soft furrows of cedar bark
the waxy leather of salal
the prick of oregon grape
the smooth cold of alder trunk
the stab of blackberry
the crucifixion of devil's club
the soft bed, feathered nest, of moss
the electric sting of nettles
the thin stiffness of snowberry stems
the rich cold clumping of this soil
            —and the thick soup of air, space

touch, touch

## October 29

sliver of moon
dips at dark
into crest
of orcas

## October 30

what creates
the allure of island
is being surrounded, enclosed, held completely
in the ever-changing mystery, the ever-deepening
allure
of water

## October 31

ferry waiting at gooseberry point
pelts of rain nattering on truck
cheerful blue steel superstructure
the three red barricade lights flashing patiently
draining, dribbling down the windshield

the raised ramp running out
to  a dull greygreen passage
surface chopped with white
rolling, rolling with long wind
and enclosing cloud

## November 1

at night
some rest
some plunder

## November 2

within the sanctuary of the otto preserve
walking the circle, the labyrinth
seduced, beguiled by breeze
          rising energy of old second growth firs
          smooth flatness of grand fir needles
          crunch and sog of footstep
          glance of nervous doe, disappearing

slow down          see          feel
removed from the other, the outside
tracing footsteps
under some spell
treading before and after, long after

*for Rebecca Rettmer*

## November 3

big alder
downed by wind blast, rot
bark still spongy, pliant, alive
a willing martyr of substrate
for mottled mosaic of lichen

nations of color, texture
on map of decay

## November 4

the curious winding estuary
encircling legoe bay
flat flat surface
held, formed by now-burnished marsh grass
blue heron a frozen fixture
waiting          perhaps
not even breathing

## November 5

hale's passage

drifting but determined fog
filtering and prisming the late morning sun
into auras and shafts and crystal spectre

like a slowly moving storm of white light
revealing the splendor of the ordinary
obscuring what we once knew and ignored

> gulls frivol
> a lone raven
> gleaning the shoreline
> dips and crawks three times
> raises and wafts toward me,
> gives a clear eyed look
> and veers off into the fog

## November 6

the water stretches out
to an indeterminate horizon
curves back overhead
in a steady grey drizzle

silently

## November 7

how seldom
i slip through
and hear
the plangent drumming
dugouts pushed into dark water
white smoke curling from
cedar longhouses warm
against the gelid hold
of hard winter,
of my hardened disregard.

## November 8

before our time
a long slow thrust and jumble
a cracking plastic crust
a patient collision of massive plates
then subsidence, erosion, leaving the stubborn
surrounded by the incessant water,
becoming island

and after our time
perhaps slowly lowering itself and drowning
or perhaps the sea recedes into ice
or perhaps the long slow thrust and jumble
pushes this ground into the sky, beyond the water,
becoming hill, mountain

and in the big picture
the long picture
this island (no matter how it's zoned) just
a quick blip

## November 9

remembering now
this season
the world is mostly dark

howling black nights
and many days only a thin
lens of grey light to the south:

muted water
dark knots of land
lowering clouds, layer upon layer

wild unwavering winds
pressing out
the weakening light

## November 10

the bio-anomaly of lummi:

a deer a deer
only from
the neck up.

the body remaining
carries splotches of color
over a white background

looks like

> a horse—pinto, paint
> appaloosa
>
> or dipped and spotted,
> an easter-egg goat

only a step, a slip away
from minotaur, unicorn
sasquatch

## November 11

clouds move into us
        grey, foreboding
        clotted and racing
larger than our lives

giving only weak
filtered light
without color

the island a hulk of
darkness caught
between the leaden wash of water
and the leaden wash of sky

time to curl in
go deep
to other light

## November 12

the way the water looks.

it was the same for
the cannery workers in the twenties
the same for crews of vancouver's ships
the same for the paddlers of the long war canoes
        bent on material goods and slaves
the same for the very first
band of human immigrants
        seeking warmth as they
        pushed south from the bering land bridge

and the same before any
human eyes, for
thousands and thousands and thousands
of years.
without us.

## November 13

the first fresh view:
	intrigue of water, cloud, sky
	enticement of shore, its critters, kelp
	the beguilement of the inner forest, paths, meadows
	the delight of this island

the everyday view:
	the same old stuff, yeah, yeah
	we look only long enough to navigate
	reassuring ourselves that things are still there
	(in a blur, becoming work, symbol, instead of being)
	the confinement of island

the older, deeper view:
	immerse in sound, smell, light, touch
	remembering water, cloud, sky are
	not words, not those *things*, but
	marvelous interplay in some pattern
	that runs in us, feeding,
	nurturing, inciting, provoking.

		this island as grounded center
		of wandering bubbling fringe
		of the universe, of the divine,
		never knowable, never the same

November 14

* This page left intentionally blank, with none of my words to warp or color or deflect the experience of this moment of your day. A gift of filterless reality, for your words.

## November 15

bushwhacking
the perfect description
breaking the lifeless limbs
squishing mosses
crumbling aged logs
on hands and knees
following the blacktail trails

behind me  a path of destruction, change
in front:
two point buck
roused from his bed
nibbles here and there
antlers curve in the ghost of last light

## November 16

dormant

leaves loosen and alight, returning to soil and root
stems and branches become brittle, stark
sap drains and coils in the cold roots

and like a seed
i enfold, harden at the edges, go in to the center
nurturing, processing, holding

the world suspends
waits, watches    through dim light
the unconscious barely breathc

and the work is to dream, just dream

## November 17

sky thickens
warps, ripples
begins to bulge
with yesterday's weather
from the far landless ocean

mt baker in black and white
the dim gentle light
holding us all in
soft cool

## November 18

outcroppings of bedrock and
erratics strewn amongst the till;
the insistent pushy blackberry,
the solid old firs, ragged but anchored in deep;
the stinging nettle thriving in disturbance—
folk on the island, character
deepened by chosen isolation
and a clear lack of anonymity
living in a confined, but very public, universe
there is nowhere to go but round and round or off—
all, somehow, making community.

## November 19

cold squish of black mud

<table><tr><td>wind beats<br>mauve tangle<br>of bare limbs<br>frantic</td><td>new water<br>bleeds<br>into buck<br>track, pools</td></tr></table>

rain last night
rain tonight

late fall.

## November 20

we kick the scatter
of frosted leaves, scrumbling
and hear within the
deep seasonal delight of change.
eyes taste the color
deep of
umber, burnt umber, bronzed umber
elemental earth
the color of soil that gravels our soul
rimed in delicate, ephemeral crystal
and let those parts of us
that need to
fall and die and melt
back unto the cold brown earth and
the rest walk on
kicking the scatter, in delight

*for Gloria Ruyle*

## November 21

six killdeer
move with wash of wave
back, forth
skittering on dainty legs
in nimble rhythm

## November 22

empty beach

stretches long to the point
            —the white rock at the end
              clean, angular
hardpacked sand disassembling to gravel wash
polite hushed waves
matia/sucia pushed far out
into gentled pink of sunset
the water
quivering slowly

I am the first here.
my footprints hard, blaring.

## November 23

snowberries
floating white planets
in a dim dripping cosmos
of rust and umber and deep
variegated grey—yet
somehow

*lush*

absolute white, presented simply
without expectation
as gifts.

## November 24

we meander the beach at midnight
suspended soft waves and moon
firs rearing black against stardrift
then someone stops, agape
look! there! and there!
we all stop.
mesmerized in delight—
phosphorescent winks in curl
of each wave
cold electric green blips
from nowhere, making
sentences of light,
enchantment

*for Joy Burns*

## November 25

wave moves to shore
gravity-sucked backwash undercuts
crest topples in
endless sliding curl

clean, perfect
neat.

## November 26

the once-white dusky grey cloud bulks
now lavender limned, infused
with slumbering salmonberry crisp crimson, auric
acid yellow, the spry exact creep of electric
orange and turquoise fade to black glitter velvet,
the sun a depthless eye of dying blood
shimmering, volatile unto the night

## November 27

the sunset is not a thing
but an action, swirling
earth rotating me away from sun
photons bouncing weirdly off
air, water vapor, dust, aeolian plankton, hubris
an interminable action, flowing
pole to pole, unceasing
across the face
of this awe-struck planet

## November 28

i can understand that perfect physics
that balance of gravity
holding earth to/from the sun

i do not understand, cannot
why we float, revolve, rotate, move

there can be no other reason
than silent, divine grace of intervention

plus—if we didn't move
we might exist
forever
in this form.
think of all
the problems
that would
cause.

## November 29

another dark dawn
pine branches swish and slap the house
rain slams and slathers the windows
long powerful rollers pound the beach

matia and sucia gone into fog
the nebulous enigmatic horizon now
just a bleary wetness of grey
advancing

## November 30

and it becomes the time to talk,
to tell stories, to pluck the
nearly-lost tatters of history,
to mend and sew them together
fabricating, harnessing, passing on.
        and from the best part of this island
        comes the calm raspy voice of age—
        "i remember when so-and-so . . ."
        "did i ever tell you . . ."
        the tales of myriad mayhem
        (in such a small space, we are all eccentrics)
we all listen, rapt
receiving wisdom, understanding, rightness
in mere intonation and gesture.
we are not just witnesses.

*for Craig Smith*

## December 1

colors build, masked by green
green dissipates, exposing

then drenched, leaching
tannin into oozing earth

leaving the empty grey veins of former leaves
muted drained stalks

water the color of cedar

## December 2

i wake to the sound of rain
steady, drenching, but clear sky overhead
low thick fog
swarming the remnant-leafed alders
in perfect condensing alchemy
wets and floods the leaf curl,
hard heavy fast drops
spattering cold splatter

shiver—stand by the fire

## December 3

late afternoon walk to village point
mt baker stunning austere in white sunlight
curled wisps of approaching front engulfing west islands
we meet and talk with others strolling, biking in the chilled light
island news
soaking in the weak sun

## December 4

fallen and crashed leaves
        hulls of worn-out machines
        scraping, etching the rock in minute ways
        freeing more hard molecules
        to seep into soil
        to fuel new leaves, more etch, new poems

## December 5

up early
not yet a glimmer of dawn
stars shot throughout
the brilliant black sky
—a rare sight here—
holding firm and
whirling in relativity—
through sleep i have
missed most of their dance
and sunblue skies have
masked the rest—
and in this cold and dark
predawn, i fill with
remorse, knowing we witness
such a small sliver

## December 6

rose hips: tiny bombs
of summer's energy:
gash of earth-blood from
blinding sun/green
now scarlet interplay

stand with your feet just right
rub and twirl these red red berries
take deep their pliant wet
hold, call forth
the coming orgasm
of spring

## December 7

the water lays on the land
the water lays on the land
          this land of island lays on the water
the water lays on the land
the water lays on the land

## December 8

kept
in the womb
of crepuscular winter light

held
in dim graygreen
close, in tight

enfolding
heart, mind
in warmth of solitude

## December 9

a mass approaches

slow, patient, immanent
a hushed power of something
trickles the sea surface

the rooted things, the trees, the rocks
look back at us,
making sure we are aware, attending

it is not a color, but a certain shading
it is not a sound, but a grounding tone
not a smell, but a dusky slowly-seething ether

not warm, not cold, but the temperature
of breath      not ours
vast, sure, ponderous

and it moves through us

## December 10

the moon in its journey
rises into ice aura
then is swallowed into
predawn swirl of mist,
cloud pulse,
tide work

## December 11

the hard cold
shrunken salal
flaccid ferns and brittle stems
everything withdrawn, muted
or crystallized, splintered into
a lifeless lattice

a snort of fogged breath
and the doe
warm under her exact hair

leaps off

## December 12

far out
on open water
wind of raw ungraspable power
feeds on the vastness
slaps and spatters the waves
into stinging frenzied spray

## December 13

close in
wind wrecking in the old firs
pushing, splintering past their flex
tearing through
their blood, ripping
the soft lovely tips
of last summer's growth,
flinging them down
to the cold trembling ground

## December 14

wavering and unwavering
merciless wind screams through the night
we begin to think, to dream
it's more than just thermodynamics

## December 15

frenzied crush of surf
on the hysterical beach
high tide and rolling chopped swells
northwest down the length of the strait
floats out all the drift logs
roll and toss and thud and scrape
flip into the swift air
pummel into the sand

a chaos of debris, pulverizing
turmoil, rearranging
this small cosmos

    above it all
    calm and holding
        like serene grey flowers
    gulls drift, nonchalant
    watching for morsels

## December 16

the next morning
it has passed and
we are held
in stillness

walking to the point, the road
    littered with the soft lovely tips of fir
    bright dismembered branches
    on the wet black pavement

we understand to breathe deeply
relieved it is not us
aware, thankful
to begin once again

## December 17

the first snow
roads are all ice
vehicles splayed everywhere

we sit safely on the ferry
mark the purser says:
no problem with traction out here

## December 18

why there are no clams:

strong northwest wind
straight down the strait
four foot swells crossing a high tide
curl savagely into the beach
churning and grinding
rock and sand and logs
in roar of power.

trading energy
          from fire
          to air
          to water
          to earth.

## December 19

after the storm
i go to the beach
          search for stones
          which have never been seen
before.
ever.

finger a few, maybe
never to be touched
again, ever.

and remember
          this sky
          this earth
          this instant
has never been before
and will never be
                    again.

it is once.

## December 20

pillows of light
hovering     holding just above
flat violet wet
under stunning blue
expanse of clear, painful sun

beyond, the white presence
of baker

in huge silence

## December 21

thick white cloud bank
sits all day just behind sucia

then late afternoon dense
snow shroud cascades down orcas

lone eagle huddles
on pt migley snag

watching

## December 22

somewhere to the south
the frazzled yellowgrey marl
of dim sun has shrunk
to its weakest.

darkness has closed in
the deep belly of grey is long, heavy

we need to know this,
to curl deep within.

and remember:
every day now
will be longer.

## December 23

predawn, cats out
sit on rocks, peer into greyness
i see, but not quite
something there, that
is more apparent
if i look away

## December 24

some days it is          dull grey   leaden purple   ashen umber
murky struggled light daubed drab
cold and deathly wet to touch

some days it is          silver   platinum   lilac/violet
etched in fine thin light, shimmering
bleeding the exact perfect nature

of winter

## December 25

matia sucia patos
the three islands to the west, the sunset view
i've walked matia and sucia, circumpiscatated patos
watched storm waves wreck in white blasts high against their fixed grit.
they are rock, real, immutable.

yet, looking through seven years of photographs
they are never the same.

sometimes large and close enough to touch, a stone's throw,
sometimes miniscule at the far edge of the seen universe;

sometimes three distinct entities
like rogue brothers, staking out their own territory and myths
and sometimes merged into a unity
a vague blue mystery of coalescence

and purple and black and violet and grey and yellow and red
and bullish and demure and hard and soft and cold
and seductive and mundane and stunning

the contrasts are more than just the dance of optics
more than just our filtered and quirky perception
it is the ever-changing, ever-absorbing breath of now
in oneness with wind, water, light and yes, our eyes, our mind

not what they are, but what they do

## December 26

minus tide

night walking on fingers
of chuckanut sandstone
at water's edge

what the mind creates
what i choose to think and feel:

softly curved fleshforms

the boulders
chunks of void
pits of black holes
surrounded by glimmering dazzle

it is all a soft breath
nuzzling
nurturing

but another reality
the one that seizes heart/mind in fear/dread

old concreted beaches, rebar rusted out
millions of years old
on a lifeless planet flying through the universe
in cold limitless
grace

the nurture in that

## December 27

seduction by water. i had to know this, to live by the sea.

it is not one thing.

my veins arise in the high country, the bleeding snowbanks
stone cold purity, the clarity of stars within a trickle
gathering, rolling and shaping the smooth lustrous cobble of memory
filtering through serene roots of old growth fir and cedar
swelling, heavy and slow and arterial in the fertile flatlands

stained from life and death, sucked into the heart of gravity

the vital work is here in the oceansea, the deep salt:
feisty liquid seed, cushion of embryonic fluid
moving to the moon and sun, curling to the spin
nurturing, flooding, giving definition to an entire planet
tempering the dead cold of space and element

with warm female rain

completing the cycle, lover's touch on desert skin
pulsing wet in searching soul
stoking the insatiable current of desire
to plunge into again and again
and call forth the marvelous swirl.

it is one thing, never the same.

## December 28

in the grey winter
we live under     and within
the undulating mammarous
darkened oozing of clouds

          above                              —way above
          the clean tufted white
          of their bright bulging backs
          swelling to the patient, patient sun

## December 29

i have had the luck and gift
to sit deeply here
exploring
a maelstrom of beauty, root, and reality
a geography of experience, consciousness and belief
immersing in
the entrancement of place.
i am profoundly grateful.

*for Bob Campbell*

## December 30

the view from this island
is the view from this mind.

the island and the mind
encircle one another
          whisper back and forth.
the island and the mind
when paying attention
          are the same.

## December 31

held here
    by the entire earth

surrounded by
    skittish, fragile beliefs
    unseen fantasy
    restless, sacred fear
    the exigent, teeming culture

we exist
    watching
    breathing
    floating

in our own exact way.
in grace. with gratitude.

Lummi Island is place like any other. You would probably be disappointed to discover that it has its share of pavement and subdivisions, growth issues, and community strife. With more people, even just curious visitors, it seems to become less of itself. My hope is that you will begin to see the place you live as I have seen Lummi Island, that you will find the poetry in your own home place. And that if your place is too far removed from its source to hold poetry, that you will strike your roots deeper and wipe some of the debris off the surface, until the poetry begins to appear.

## Acknowledgments

I would like to thank all who had a hand in the genesis and final form of this manuscript: the early Chinese poets and their descendants, Carole Smidt, Kent Morse, John Wright, Jillian Froebe, poets@risk, Maya Allen-Gallegos, and J. I. Kleinberg.

March 27 was previously published in Volume 15 of the *Chrysalis Reader*. November 18 was selected as a winning poem in the 2006 Sue C.Boynton Poetry Contest; May 13 was selected in the 2007 Sue C. Boynton Poetry Contest.